Fell Pony

Fell Ponies are a native of the North of England and are thought to have roamed in the old counties of Cumberland and Westmorland for centuries.

As industry developed, ponies were used to transport iron, copper and lead ores from the mines in the north-west of England to smelting works in Newcastle and carry coal on the return journey. Ponies were used in the collieries into the twentieth century, underground if there was sufficient height and above ground to haul machinery and dairy produce to the towns from the colliery farms above the pits. Ponies were also used in pack pony trains and for postal services which were necessary for the remote communities.

Pedigrees of the Fell ponies were recorded by breeders in the late nineteenth century and show classes for 'Fell Ponies' were held at Hesket New Market show in 1894 and at Shap in 1895. The first fell ponies registered were entered in the Polo and Riding Pony Stud Book in 1898.

The Fell Pony Society was formed in 1922 to keep pure the old breed of pony. In the 1950's there was an increase in the popularity of riding for pleasure which guaranteed the future of the Fell Pony at the time.

The height should not exceed 14 hands (142.2cm) and colours of black, brown, bay and grey are permitted. Chestnuts, skewbalds and piebalds are not allowed. A white star is permitted and a small amount of white on or below the fetlock is permitted. Excess white markings are discouraged although ponies with such markings are eligible for registration.

The head is small and well defined in outline, the forehead is broad and tapers to the nose. Nostrils are large and eyes prominent, bright and intelligent. Ears are small, well-formed and neatly set on to the head.

The throat and jaw are fine with no signs of coarseness. The neck is proportional to the head and body, giving a good length of rein. The neck is also strong but not too heavy and stallions have a moderate crest.

Shoulders are well laid back and sloping, withers are not too fine but not loaded. The shoulder blade is long and the muscles are well developed.

The back is strong with a good outline. The pony is deep bodied and muscular and short-coupled with a well set on tail and square hind quarters.

Feet are a good size with blue horn, open at the heel and well-shaped. Pasterns are not too long, forelegs are not tied in at the elbow and knees are large and well-formed. The Fell Pony has short cannon bones with good flat bone below the knees (at least 8 inches) and the forearm is muscular.

Hind legs are muscular with good thighs and second thighs, hocks are well let down and well defined, with plenty of bone below. Ponies should not be sickle or cow-hocked.

The action of the Fell Pony is smart and straight at the walk, well balanced at the trot, flexing at the hock and moving from the shoulder. Hind legs should not be too close or too wide apart. The pony moves with a good pace, bringing the hocks well under the body.

The Fell Pony should be hardy and have good pony characteristics but also be lively, alert in appearance and have good bone.

The Fell Pony is suitable for adults and children and makes an ideal family pony suitable for hacking, general riding and driving.

www.ingramcontent.com/pod-product-compliance
Lightning Source LLC
Chambersburg PA
CBHW050423290526
45786CB00003B/1379